21st Century Skills **INNOVATION LIBRARY**

UNOFFICIAL **GUIDES**

MINDSTORMS: Level 4

Peacntree

CHERRY LAKE PUBLISHING • ANN ARBOR, MICHIGAN

by Rena Hixon

CHERRY
LAKE
Publishing

A Note to Adults: Please review the instructions for the activities in this book before allowing children to do them. Be sure to help them with any activities you do not think they can safely complete on their own.

A Note to Kids: Be sure to ask an adult for help with these activities when you need it. Always put your safety first!

Published in the United States of America by Cherry Lake Publishing
Ann Arbor, Michigan
www.cherrylakepublishing.com

Reading Adviser: Marla Conn, Read With Me Now
Photo Credits: Cover and page 1, ©PRNewsFoto/LEGO MINDSTORMS;
all others, Rena Hixon

Library of Congress Cataloging-in-Publication Data
Hixon, Rena, author.
Mindstorms. Level 4 / by Rena Hixon.
   pages cm. — (Unofficial guides)
Audience: Grades 4 to 6.
Summary: "Explore advanced techniques in Mindstorms, from programming
a series of movements to collecting and analyzing robot data."— Provided by
publisher.
Includes bibliographical references and index.
ISBN 978-1-63470-527-1 (lib. bdg.) — ISBN 978-1-63470-647-6 (pbk.) —
ISBN 978-1-63470-587-5 (pdf) — ISBN 978-1-63470-707-7 (ebook)
1. LEGO Mindstorms toys—Juvenile literature. 2. Robotics—Juvenile literature.
3. Computer programming—Juvenile literature. 4. Gyroscopes—Juvenile
literature. I. Title.
TJ211.H59 2016
629.8'92—dc23   2015036041

Cherry Lake Publishing would like to acknowledge the work of The Partnership
for 21st Century Skills. Please visit www.p21.org for more information.

Printed in the United States of America
Corporate Graphics
January 2016

Century Skills INNOVATION LIBRARY

Contents

Chapter 1

Some Useful Tools

Welcome to Level 4! By now you should know how to build and program a basic robot. Your programs should be able to accomplish more than one goal at a time, such as following a line and stopping when the sonar detects something within a range. You should know how to use the ultrasonic sensor, the light sensor, the infrared sensor, and the touch sensor. You should also know the difference between the "Wait For", "Switch", and various sensor **icons**. With that knowledge, you are ready for this book.

Let's start out by looking at some helpful tools in the EV3 software. One tool that is extremely useful when learning to program is the "Show Context Help" option. You can find it by clicking on the "Help" menu. When it is selected, a brief explanation will show up on-screen every time you select an icon. There is also an option labeled "More Information" on most of the explanations. If you click this, it will open a separate window that gives you even more detailed information about the icon. If you have questions about how an icon works, be sure to check this out.

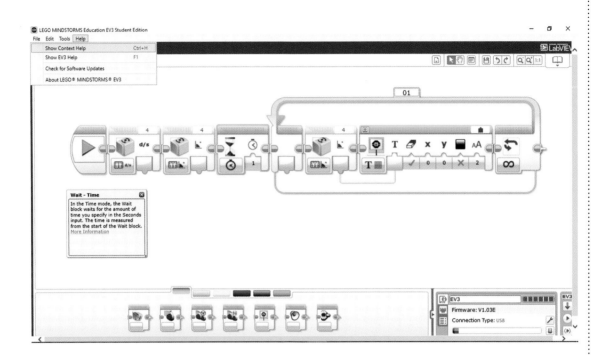

Another helpful tool is the Memory Browser. One way to access this is to click the icon in the second box to the left in the lower corner of the screen. It looks kind of like a cake with a dark bottom layer. It is underneath the wrench. You can also click on the "Tools" menu and select "Memory Browser". Either of these actions will bring up a Memory Browser window. On the left side of the window is a bar graph. This graph indicates how much **memory** you are using on the EV3 brick. On the right side, it will show all the programs currently loaded on the brick.

Simplifying the Programming Process

If you ever decide to start learning about other programming languages, you will find that they all have features similar to the blocks in Mindstorms. In other languages, these are called functions, routines, or methods. It is very common to put code that is used more than once into a function. This function can then be "called" from elsewhere in the program. This eliminates the need to write duplicate code in a program. Functions are also used to group together code that performs a certain task, just like blocks.

Occasionally when you are downloading and running a lot of different programs, you might get an error message stating that you are out of memory. When this happens, you can use the Memory Browser to remove programs from the EV3 brick. This won't delete them forever from your computer. However, it will create free space on the EV3 for new programs. If you ever need to use the old programs, just open them in the EV3 software and load them onto your brick again.

In the Memory Browser, select the program you want to remove by clicking on its name. It will then highlight the things that you can do with that program. The option we are interested in is "Delete". You will have to select each program you want to remove and then select "Delete" to get rid of them. Notice that there are some programs on the robot that cannot be deleted. They include the programs in the "Applications" folder and the program titled "BrkProg_SAVE". These are programs the EV3 needs to run correctly.

Your Memory Browser will look different than the one shown below. This is because you likely have a completely different list of programs on your EV3.

Another useful tool is the **firmware** updater. To find it, click the "Tools" menu and select "Firmware Update". There are rare occasions when your robot

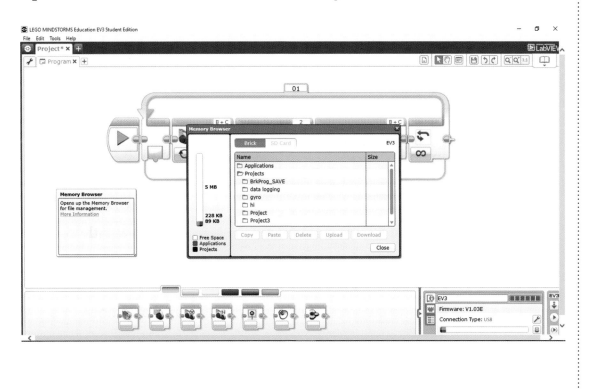

may start acting a lot differently than you expect it to. When this happens, you can try updating the firmware to fix it. You will need to select the firmware version under "Available Firmware Files". Then you can select "Download" to update the firmware.

Updating the firmware is not something you want to do on a regular basis. It will not harm your EV3 in any way, but it will erase all the programs you have loaded onto the brick. This means you will need to download them again. You only need to update

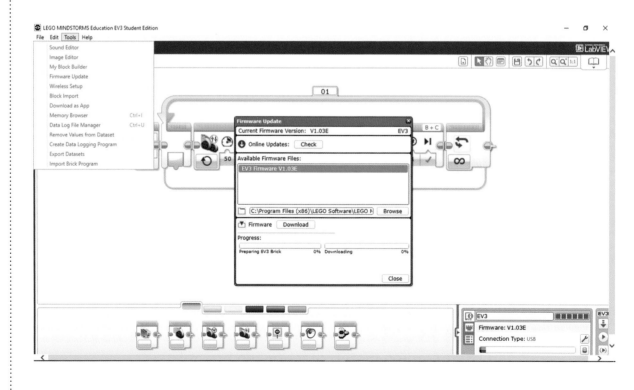

the firmware if odd things are happening with your robot and you can find no explanation for the strange behavior. For example, imagine your program is supposed to be following a line. You have made absolutely sure that you are running the correct program. The light sensor is on the correct port and plugged in, yet it will not turn on. This might be solved by downloading new firmware.

If you would like to draw a picture to display on the EV3 screen as your robot moves around, you can use the Image Editor. Open it by clicking on the "Tools" menu and selecting "Image Editor". You can use the icons on the left-hand side of the screen to draw an image. Use the folder at the top left to save the image. The images you draw in the Image Editor are only available for the project where you save them. If you want to use them in different projects, you will have to copy them.

Once you have created and saved an image, close the Image Editor and go to your program. Select a "Display" icon and choose "Image". Click on the white block at the top right and you should see the name of your saved image. You can select it and display it wherever you like in your program. For example, you might place a "Display" icon to show an image on the EV3 every time the robot detects an object in front of it.

The last tool we'll look at is called My Block Builder. When you start writing more complex programs, they can get very large. This makes it more difficult to figure out where you should put new icons. Thankfully, My Block Builder lets you divide your programs into smaller chunks. Each chunk becomes its own special icon called a block. You can arrange blocks and add other icons just as usual, but your program will look a lot simpler on-screen.

In this example, we will make a block using the code for a line-follow that stops when the sonar sensor detects something less than 5 inches (12.7 centimeters) away. Highlight the code that you want to be the block. Be sure that it is all blue. Do not include the "Start" icon. Once the code is highlighted, click the "Tools" menu and select "My Block Builder". A new window will pop up. It will have a space where you can enter the name of your block. Let's call it "LineFollowSon" for now. In the description box, you can type a short explanation that will help you remember what the block does.

Above the name and description is the block. You can select any of the icons in the bottom half of the window to be part of your block. You can use the + sign to add or edit parameters. Parameters are **inputs** into the block. If there are inputs that you want to use, you can add a parameter and then use a wire to connect something to your block. Once your block is done, click on "Finish".

When you click "Finish", you will see the new block in your program in place of the old code. Your program should now be a lot easier to read. If you want to change your block, you can double-click on its icon. This will open another program window titled with the name you gave the block. You can modify the program and save it. The changes will apply to the program where your block is used.

You can create multiple blocks and use them in
your program. Your main program could even be
built entirely from blocks! Remember that each block
represents a program that can be modified. If you
modify the program, the way your block functions is
changed. You can find all the blocks you create under
the light-blue tab at the bottom of the screen. This
allows you to drag them into your program just like
any other icon.

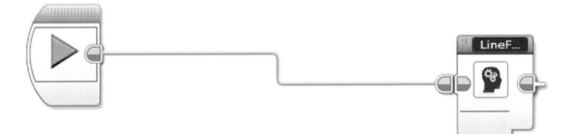

Chapter 2

Multitasking

You might want to create a program that can **execute** more than one task at a time. When you do this, you must be careful that the tasks do not conflict with each other. Suppose you want to program your robot to go through a maze. While it is going through the maze, you would like it to show the distances that the sonar is reading on the EV3 display. These two tasks would not conflict with each other as long as they are using the sonar sensor in the same way. For example, as long as the sonar is measuring inches and displaying inches, there would be no conflict. But if the sonar is being used to measure inches and display centimeters, there could be a conflict. This could cause your robot to function incorrectly.

To execute more than one task at a time, pull a wire down from the "Start" icon to another block of icons. This means you will have two separate wires coming out of the start block to two different sets of icons. In the program shown here, the top set of icons

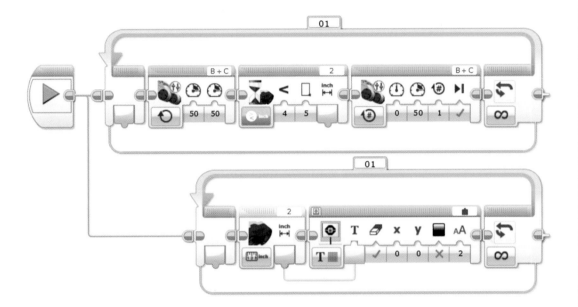

tells a robot to avoid objects. The bottom set of icons tells the EV3 to display the value of the sonar sensor.

Sometimes you might want your robot to check the conditions of two sensors at a time to see if both sensor conditions are true before exiting a loop. For example, you might want to put two touch sensors on your robot and program it to stop only if both are touched.

You can use **logic** and nested "Switch" icons to accomplish this. Grab a "Variable" icon from the red bar to start your program. Select "write–logic" on the icon. In the white box at the top right, select "Add Variable" and give it a name. We will use "ts press" in the example. The variable's value should be set to "false".

Next, connect a "Switch" icon for your first touch sensor. On the true side of the switch, use another "Switch" icon to check your other touch sensor. Add another "Variable" icon on the true side of this second "Switch" icon. Set it to "write–logic". Make sure "ts press" is in the white box in the top right

Multitasking will allow you to create robots that use several sensors at once.

corner. Change the value on the icon to "true". In the loop control, select "Logic". Grab another "Variable" icon, but this time set it to "read–logic". Again, make sure "ts press" is in the white box. Connect a wire from the **output** of this "Variable" icon to the input of the "Loop" icon. This will cause the loop to continue until both touch sensors are pressed.

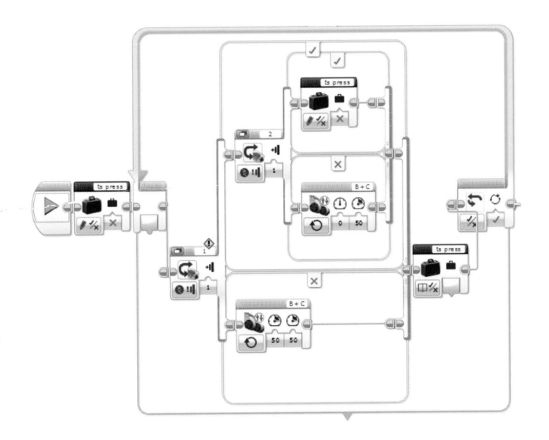

Chapter 3

The Gyro Sensor

If you are using an EV3 educational kit, you have probably noticed that there is a sensor we haven't used yet. This is the gyro sensor. If you do not have one, you can purchase it separately. However, you will need to download a special set of icons to use it with the EV3 software. For instructions, visit *http://robotsquare.com/2014/06/25/ tutorial-gyro-ultrasonic-sensor-ev3-home-edition/*.

The gyro sensor has two red arrows on its top side with a red dot between them. This sensor can measure angle and rate. This means it can determine which direction your robot is tilted and how fast it is moving. In this book, we will focus only on angle measurements. Be sure to mount your sensor **parallel** to your robot to ensure accurate measurements.

The gyro sensor is more difficult to use than the other sensors. This is partly because it is very sensitive. If you randomly plug the gyro sensor into your robot and try to take readings using the Port View, you might notice a lot of "drift." This means it will appear as if the sensor values are increasing randomly. To minimize

Gyros in the Sky

Remote-controlled quadcopters have become popular in recent years. These flying toys rely heavily on gyro sensors. A gyro can detect the angle at which the quadcopter is flying. It uses that information to adjust the copter's angle and keep it from crashing.

drift, you must hold the sensor completely still as you connect it to the EV3 brick. This is explained in the general help section of the EV3 software.

If you are experiencing drift, unplug the gyro sensor from the EV3. Keep the sensor and brick perfectly still for at least three seconds. Now plug it back in. You should now be able to use the sensor to take readings.

If you go to Port View right after plugging the gyro sensor in, you should see a reading of zero. If you rotate your robot 90 degrees, you should see 90 degrees on the display. However, this doesn't always work perfectly. There might still be some drift even if you kept the sensor motionless as you connected it.

You can also have drift problems while using the gyro sensor in programs. One possible solution to the problem is to change the sensor's mode from "angle" to "rate" and make sure that your robot is absolutely still for three seconds while the change takes place.

You can do this with the simple program shown below. There can still be some drift even when you do this, but it should be much less than without it.

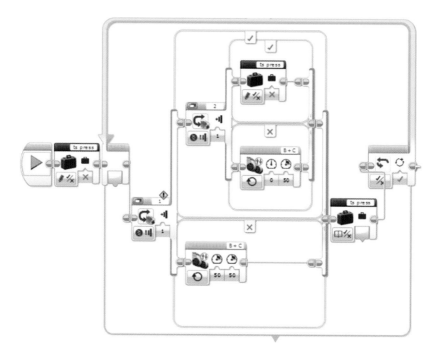

Assuming you get the gyro sensor to work well, you can use it to help your robot make measured turns to drive along a specific path. Suppose you want to make your robot drive in a square path. To do this, you would want it to drive forward a certain distance, turn 90 degrees, and repeat the process three more times.

Do you have a smartphone, tablet, or laptop that changes the direction of the screen depending on how you hold the device? If so, you are holding a gyro sensor in your hand. The gyro sensor is used to detect the angle at which you are holding your device. The device then uses this information to make sure the display is always right-side up no matter which way you are holding it.

See if you can write the program yourself before you check out the solution.

The beginning of the program should include the code shown above for preventing drift. To program the robot to drive in a square, you will need to repeat the same motion four times. You can use a loop to do this. Add a "Loop" icon to your program. Select "Count" on the loop control and set the number to 4. Inside the loop, program the robot to drive forward for a set distance. In this example, we will use one rotation. Now program the robot to start turning. Add a "Wait For" icon and wait for the gyro sensor to change by 90 degrees. Then set the robot's motors to stop. This will cause the robot to pause slightly before starting the loop over again. That's it! You should have a robot that can drive in

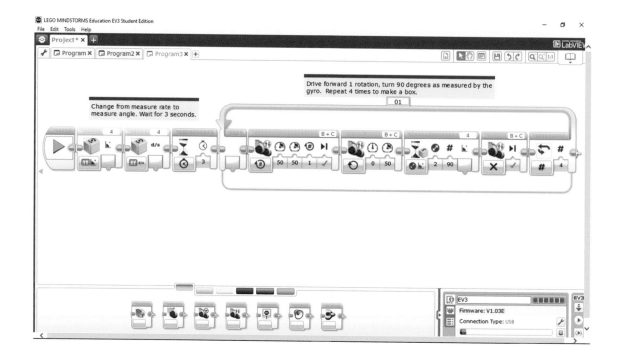

a square. Above is the program solution for your reference.

Another way you can use the gyro sensor in the "angle" mode is to detect if the robot starts to climb. In order to determine if your robot is climbing, you will need to mount the top of your gyro sensor **perpendicular** to your robot.

For example, try making a ramp by propping up a board or some other flat, sturdy object at an angle.

Drive your robot toward it. When your robot starts going up the board, the gyro sensor will detect the change in angle. Maybe the robot was following a line and the line goes up the board partway before curving back down. Instead of following the line, you want the robot to drive straight up the board. You could accomplish that with the gyro sensor. The program given here drives straight until the gyro detects an angle greater than 10 degrees. You can replace the drive forward with a line-follow or any other task of your choosing.

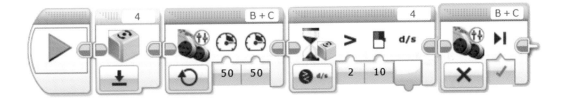

Chapter 4

Data Logging

The educational version of the EV3 software includes a powerful tool called data logging. Data logging can be performed in its own window. It can also be included in programs to become an even more powerful **debugging** tool.

Start by plugging your EV3 into your computer. Click on the "File" menu and select "Add Experiment". Data logging is used to graph values from the EV3 sensors. You can do this with the EV3 connected, or you can use data logging icons in a program to collect data as your robot runs. This data can be downloaded to the graph and viewed later.

Once you plug your EV3 into your computer, all the sensors that are connected will be displayed automatically. In the section labeled "Sensor Setup", you can use the red x to remove any sensors you don't want to view. Next to each sensor, there is also a bar where you can change what you want each sensor to detect. For example, if your color sensor is detecting reflected light, you can select the bar next to the color sensor and change it to detect color. A third bar shows the port to which your sensor is connected. A fourth bar shows a color. This indicates the color of the line that will appear on the graph.

In the bottom left portion of the screen, there is a box labeled "Experiment Units Setup". Here you can change the duration and rate of the data capture. Notice that changing the duration will change the labels on the graph's x-axis (the line going from side to side). Because the durations you are observing are so short, you will not see much of a change in the data by changing the duration. On the y-axis (the line going from top to bottom), you should notice that the labels show the possible values for each sensor that is attached.

At the top right side of the screen are different tools that you can use for the graph. One of the things you can do is to stop taking data while the EV3 is plugged in. If you move your cursor over these icons, the one called "Stop Oscilloscope Mode" will stop showing samples and clear the screen. The tool labeled "Comment" will allow you to put comments on your graphs. "Screen Shot" allows you to save a picture of everything currently on the screen. "Save Project" allows you to save the project you are working on. There are also "Zoom In" and "Zoom Out" buttons for your graph.

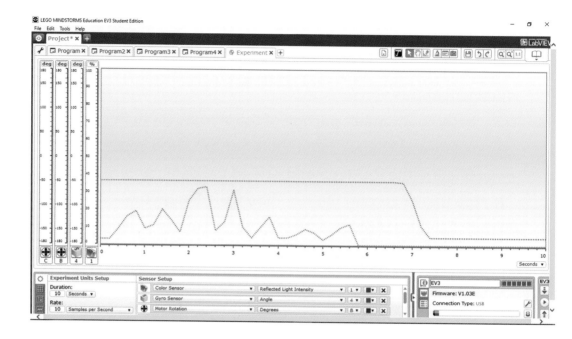

So far, we have looked at what you can do from the experiment screen. But as mentioned earlier, data logging can also be done while you are running a program. This is done by putting data logging commands into your program.

An easy example is to write a line-follow program that ends when the sonar sensor detects something within a few inches of it. You should be able to write this program based on the knowledge you gained from previous books in this series. Once you are done, you can add the data logging commands to the program. The "Data Logging" icons are under the bright-blue tab at the bottom of the screen. Drag one into your program. The icon has a white block at the

A Robot's-Eye View

Have you ever wanted to see what your robot "sees" as it travels along? Data logging can allow you to see what the sensors are detecting as your robot is running. You can set up data logging for your motors and all your sensors. This can give you a complete view of everything your robot is sensing and doing as it follows a program.

top left-hand corner. The default value in that block is "MyData". This will be the name of the data set that is generated as your program runs. You can change the name to what you want it to be. At the lower right corner of the icon, you can select which sensor you want to collect data from.

There are two input values on this icon. The first one is rate, and the second one is rate unit. The meaning of the rate value differs depending on the rate unit. If the rate unit is 0, then the rate will be samples per second. If the rate unit is 1, then the rate will be seconds between samples. You can choose a rate anywhere from 1 to 1,000. If the rate unit is 0 and rate is 50, then 50 samples will be taken every second. If the rate unit is 1 and the rate is 1, then a sample will be taken once every second.

You can log the information from more than one sensor at a time. There is a + sign on the right side of the icon. Click it to add another sensor to be monitored.

You must use another "Data Logging" icon at the end of the program and set it to end data logging to successfully capture a data set. The name specified in the icon at the end of the program must be the same name given in the icon at the beginning of the program. Below is a simple data logging program. Run it to capture a data set.

After you have run the program, you can take a look at the data it collected. First, go back to the experiment screen. You can do this by selecting the + sign near the top left corner of the screen and choosing "Experiment". While your robot is connected, it will automatically start showing you the value of the sensors

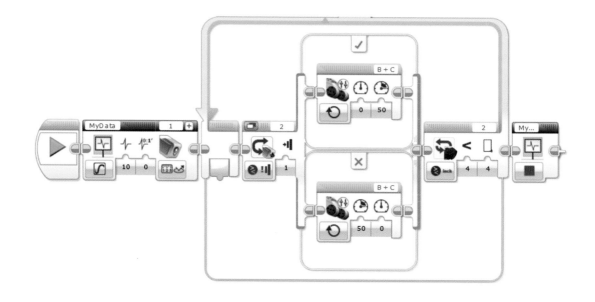

that you have connected. Stop the oscillator to turn this off. Now click the "Upload" arrow in the lower left part of the screen. A screen called "Data File Log Manager" will appear. There will be a list of the programs loaded on the EV3. Find the name of your data logging program and double-click. Now you should see a file with the name of the data set that you captured in your program. Click on the data set and then select "Import" from the lower part of the screen. The data set will then be loaded into a graph. Close the "Data File Log Manager" window so you can see the data.

Data logging will help you understand what your sensor is seeing while it is on your robot. This can possibly help you find problems with a program by allowing you to see what your sensors are actually detecting, rather than what you think they are detecting.

Hopefully, you have learned a lot about using the EV3 software in this series of books. We have focused mostly on using the programming language and not on how to build robots. However, you can build almost anything you can think of using Mindstorms. Then you can use your programming skills to make them move and react to their environment. Most importantly, have fun!

Glossary

debugging (dee-BUH-ging) finding and fixing errors in a program

execute (EK-suh-kyoot) carry out a planned action

firmware (FURM-wair) software that is built into a piece of hardware, enabling it to function

icons (EYE-kahnz) graphic symbols on a computer screen that represent programs, functions, or files

inputs (IN-puts) places where information is fed into a device

logic (LAH-jik) a particular way of thinking

memory (MEM-uh-ree) the part of a computer in which instructions and information are stored

output (OUT-put) information produced by a computer

parallel (PAR-uh-lel) staying the same distance from each other and never crossing or meeting

perpendicular (pur-puhn-DIK-yuh-lur) a line that is at right angles to another line or to a surface

Find Out More

BOOKS

Benedettelli, Daniele. *The Lego Mindstorms EV3 Laboratory: Build, Program, and Experiment with Five Wicked Cool Robots!* San Francisco: No Starch Press, 2014.

Park, Eun Jung. *Exploring Lego Mindstorms EV3: Tools and Techniques for Building and Programming Robots.* Indianapolis: Wiley, 2014.

WEB SITE

Lego Mindstorms: Build a Robot
www.lego.com/en-us/mindstorms/build-a-robot
Check out instructions for building other Mindstorms robots.

Index

About the Author

Rena Hixon received a bachelor's degree in computer science from the University of Missouri–Rolla (now Missouri University of Science and Technology). She also earned a doctorate in electrical engineering from Wichita State University. She worked as a software design engineer for 11 years and has taught computer science classes at Wichita State for more than 13 years. In 2004, Rena and her husband started a Lego robotics club for homeschooled students. Its aim is to teach engineering principles, emphasizing math and science, to children. Rena has also taught her own Lego robotics camps for 12 years as well as camps at Missouri S&T for several years.